CALIFORNIA HOMES II

STUDIO WILLIAM HEFNER

CALIFORNIA HOMES II

In loving memory of Kazuko

Kazuko delighted in
bringing beauty into people's lives.

7	INTRODUCTION **THE NEW CALIFORNIA**
11	TROUSDALE
35	ROMERO CANYON
63	BEVERLY HILLS
91	CANYON FARMHOUSE
117	WILSHIRE
135	NEW LONDON
171	PALISADES RANCH
199	HOT SPRINGS
233	AVIGNON
261	FLIGHT
291	BIOGRAPHY
293	ACKNOWLEDGMENTS
294	PROJECT CREDITS

INTRODUCTION
THE NEW CALIFORNIA

This is my second book that carries the title California Homes. The first book, published in 2013, documented an earlier series of houses that I designed and built in southern California, in the Los Angeles area in particular. And while southern California is not the only place that I build houses, it does occupy a fascination for me. It's the anchor of my work and it is home.

Over the past three decades, I've been privileged to design houses in all the historical and modern styles that populate this cinematic landscape of canyons, palisades, and grand old Hollywood neighborhoods. I've welcomed new opportunities to work in more country and rustic idioms, on larger sites, with more land to play with. The projects overall have gotten bigger—if not always in size, then certainly in ambition. They're more challenging in site planning and construction; in the sculpting of buildings to take best advantage of landscape and views, while being beautiful forms themselves. Gardens, pools, outbuildings, and native land restoration have become more central to each home. I've been able to draw on the strengths of a team with more specialized expertise in craft, engineering, and horticulture, allowing us to continually push the boundaries of what we can do—not just aesthetically, but also materially and technically.

Most interesting, though, has been the growing interest in more adventurous modern design among our clients and in the culture here generally. This is not just an appetite for European modern classicism, or the quintessential midcentury architecture of Los Angeles. The desired houses are about individualism, luxury, and bespoke character, even as they prize a kind of simplicity. They express something quite local, influenced by California's abundant beauty, iconic geographies, environmental sensitivity, and, of course, the sensational climate and light; virtually all are instilled with the DNA of indoor-outdoor living. This kind of house may fall under the umbrella of "contemporary", though I prefer to think of our work as a new modern. It's referential but it has less revival, less genre, in it. Oftentimes we create a hybrid that's more traditional on the outside, with the modern on the inside.

In Los Angeles as well as the countryside, another phenomenon is that more people from outside the area are coming here to build holiday homes. That, too, has affected the sense of play, internationalism, and cultural preference that we are afforded when creating California homes. Overall, there is an exciting new feeling of collaborative risk worth taking, to work outside of comfort zones and prior norms.

The local design community has been ripe for this evolution. And it's yielded a new generation of homes for us in a very short period of time. We've gotten more sophisticated, more serious in a sense.

The houses are more authored, the clients more creative. In their way, both are more experimental. Anything feels possible, every time we start a new project. And that's a great place to work from.

At their best, all these houses draw something essential forward from modernist principles of exquisite detail and natural form. They are simple in the sense of being pure and restful. But they are of now—and often incredibly complex—in their specificity, technology, and priorities. This is the type of very refined, very custom home that we make, regardless of era or typology.

The houses continue to span and stretch traditional, modern, and country architecture, reflecting the range of our clients and the studio. Looking at them as a group, I'd like to think they've begun to have their own form language that draws on all my interests, from European historical traditions to Japanese design and culture, to my years here in California, developing my practice. They include family homes informed by what I've learned as a parent; generational homes that connect past to present; homes for collectors and creatives; and, radical changes of scene for people who are simplifying or starting a new stage of life. They're elegant in any number of ways, but they're alike in being quite relaxed and welcoming. And while this work represents a certain California spirit—a free spirit, you could say—I see the same currents affecting houses that we're building in the Pacific Northwest and the Mountain West, London, and New York.

So—upon this growth, it seemed time for a new book. Books themselves are a labor of love and a compression of what is a many-years-long process into a few select pages and pictures. That's as interesting a culmination to me as in any design process. I hope that the homes collected in this book offer up an interesting sequel, with some insight into what it means to create spaces that feel like California today. Most of all, I hope that the book shares the spirit of the wonderful people for whom these houses were made. Without them and their partnership, these places would not be homes, and this adventure would not be possible.

Author's note:

This book is a record of the twenty years that my late wife, Kazuko Hoshino, and I worked together. Kazuko brought grace, talent, and her extraordinary spirit to the studio and to many of these homes. Her influence will always live on in our work and will, I believe, continue to enrich our clients' lives for years to come.

TROUSDALE

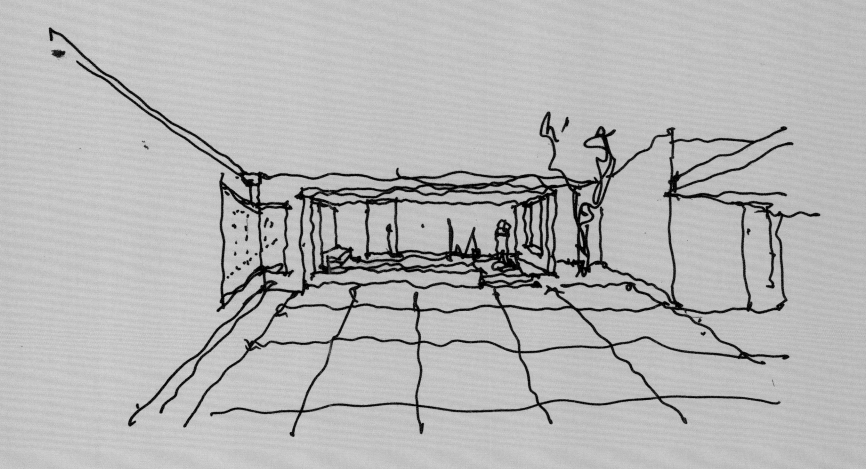

For this Los Angeles native, an avid art collector, the search for the right home began in his admiration for iconic California Case Study and midcentury houses. Over time he'd been looking for a vintage property to renovate, but even the finest Case Study houses can be quite small and have low ceilings. Few had enough space for his art.

The solution was to find a site with dramatic views and sunny exposures, and build a house inspired by the clean lines and elementality of Case Study style. We came upon a special lot in the hills above Beverly Hills, within a neighborhood of celebrated midcentury architectural houses. The new home shares their period resonance and single-story structure, though in updated, refined materials, and with higher, brighter spaces. These adaptations make the house more generous and open, and let the rooms hold up to the large paintings in the client's collection.

For the building, I wanted to use a limited palette of classic finishes that would feel right out of a Case Study house. Warm walnut offsets milk-white terrazzo floors, gallery white walls, and marble. Split-face limestone and dense ipe wood wrap from the exterior into the interiors, adding a rich dimension as they blur the lines between inside and outside.

The entrance hall bridges two pavilion-style wings and screens the front of the house for privacy. The scale of this space lets it function as a main art gallery. Skylights with diffusers filter ambient light into the hall and the rooms on its other side. This soft light overhead allows us to protect the art without having to rely too much on artificial light sources or many more fixtures.

The main body of the house intentionally opens to the southwest, so that every room has a panoramic vista, all the way to the ocean. With large, retractable glass doors, this side also opens physically to the outdoors, expanding the living area of the house. A large great room occupies the center of the plan with a prime view of the city. At forty feet long, it includes seating and dining areas and a bar, all inviting the room to be used day into night. There is a parallel open space for the kitchen and breakfast area, also looking onto the view and the pool. On the other side of the great room, a sequestered master suite is set down a few steps, with a glass corner that opens directly to the pool—a kind of world within the world of the house.

Throughout, the cabinetry and furnishings that we designed are of the same high detail and style, so that there's little division between fixtures and furniture. The newly made shares a character with the vintage pieces we sourced, punctuated in just a few places with vivid color. We let most of the flourish come from the art. Together, these select ingredients allow fewer elements to fill the rooms with uncluttered, modern tailoring.

Opposite Sculptural planting beds become living extensions of the house. The front entrance was built with a series of reveals through geometric forms. At the pond, we made a call during construction to open through the end wall in order to frame a beautiful tree on the other side.

Above In an homage to Case Study houses, a terrazzo path to the front door is suspended over a narrow pond. The low profiles of the auto court are an extension of the façade, with a carport typical of midcentury homes. Split-faced limestone updates the rough canyon stone often used in architecture of the period.

Following A glass-walled corner brings a courtyard view inside the front entry. To the right is the main gallery. The office is on the left. All the doors in the house are made floor to ceiling, in American walnut with a special, tinted natural stain. The idea of a ceiling-height door comes from the midcentury period but here the scale is taller and bolder.

Above We sourced and restored the vintage Italian rosewood dining table; the rosewood chairs were refitted with black saddle leather. Extending the Italian character, race-car-red leather was chosen for the stools at the bar as an accent. We knew the room, and the surrounding art, could handle the color.

Opposite Floor-to-ceiling glass doors in the great room are designed to retract, so that the interior can freely join the covered loggia outside. Through this opening, bright southern light plays across the space in wavelike patterns.

Following A vintage chair refurbished in buff glove leather sits casually in front of the fireplace in the great room. The fireplace's seamless limestone cladding rises twelve and a half feet—a minimalist translation of Case Study materiality. The narrow, blonde firebrick lining the box of the fireplace is characteristic of the period.

Overleaf A primary wish of the owner was that the house would have an easy indoor–outdoor functionality. The architecture complies by seamlessly opening the main interiors to the loggia and the pool. The rooms remain sheltered from the sun while becoming part of this extended outdoor living space.

Above The open kitchen and breakfast area extends from the family room. We designed the custom steel-and-maple table to be bracketed to the wall, so that the form has a lightness. The kitchen island is made entirely of quartz stone that contrasts with the walnut cabinetry and wainscoting. The Italian deckled glass mosaic wall was hand-patterned and hand-fabricated for the house.

Opposite Split-faced limestone wraps the family room from the outside in. A specimen Dracaena tree sourced from points south adds age to the landscape and mixes with other native succulents by the pool. The gardens are planted in these formations with a nod to the local desert terrain of the 1940s and 1950s, when Case Study houses were first being built.

Following A custom steel-and-teak pergola invites poolside lounging in the shade. This is the prettiest spot on the property from which to enjoy the sunset and panoramas east to west.

Opposite Polished terrazzo floors and reflective artworks multiply the light in the hallway to the master suite. Poised to overlook the pool and the view, a vintage Eames chair and ottoman seem to float in the space. The intention was to create the feeling of being among the clouds.

Above We deliberately lowered the master bedroom a few steps to gain taller ceilings and to meet the grade of the terrace around the pool. The modern, cantilevered fireplace is a soulful gesture in a bedroom; tucking it into a corner allowed us to leave the balance of space open to maximize the view. The bed platform and headboard with integral nightstands is our design, made in saddle leather and veneer.

Above (left) The master bathroom shower is partitioned with a transparent glass divider, so that it feels open to the room. Calacatta marble slabs are bookmatched for dramatic pattern across the full space, including at the sinks and surrounding the bathtub. **(right)** A lady's vanity cabinet sits across from the sinks. For a lighter feel, this cabinetry is executed in bleached, rift-cut oak, with matching leather pulls and a custom stool. The sconces are Italian.

Opposite I've always liked how midcentury houses tend to have a garden off the bathroom. In that spirit, the master bathroom has a glass wall that looks onto its own garden. Bamboo-like plum pine provides a feathery hedge for privacy. A custom marble-and-zebrawood cabinet with freestanding mirrors provides storage at the double sinks.

Following The master bedroom opens to the pool. This configuration was designed to make it easy for the owner to do early morning laps, with steps descending into the water directly outside the bedroom. Facing west, the master suite has extraordinary views to Santa Monica Bay and Catalina Island beyond. Sunsets here are magical.

ROMERO CANYON

Kazuko and I first started coming to Montecito on our way up and down the coast from Big Sur. At one point we were seriously thinking about building a place up north, but Kazuko was pregnant with our son Koji at the time. So, we began wondering about this countryside closer to Los Angeles as an option, and we looked for a long time.

The property we fell in love with was not large, at just over an acre. But it had striking views of the surrounding mountains and a number of amazing California live oak trees, most over 200 years old. A small house and stable from the 1940s weren't salvageable, but they gave the land more history.

The home we envisioned was similar to a compound, consisting of a group of easy, neighboring structures. We wanted to feel like we were on vacation, with outbuildings for activities and guests, and ample space to be outside. Modern, but also natural and local.

We arranged these buildings in a loose quadrangle around a central pool and lawn, all pushed out to the edges of the property so that we'd have the greatest amount of outdoor living space in the middle. Some of the structures are made of wood, others of golden Santa Barbara sandstone; we discovered our own abundant supply of the stone while digging the foundations on the property. A large wood deck connects the main house to the outdoors. Facing the deck, huge sliding glass doors erase the line between what's inside and what's outside.

The wings of the main house are joined in an L-shape by glazed breezeways. Two flanking stone buildings include a great room with the kitchen, and then a billiard room. Turned 90 degrees, the bedroom wing is clad in wood. The materials and the low, quiet profile of the buildings let the architecture merge organically into the wild, surrounding landscape.

The great room is where we spend most of our time. We wanted the experience of being all together in one space, especially in terms of having the kitchen there. The room has the rustic echo of a lodge, with its wood beam cathedral ceilings, cedar doors, and a tall, stone fireplace. All the interiors fall into this same material range of stained cedarwood with honed marble, brushed limestone, and burnished brass. Colors are intentionally muted and natural. We used midcentury light fixtures and vintage modern furnishings throughout to make it all feel classic.

The priority of outdoor living at this house means we do enjoy the gardens and the pool every day, whenever we are here. For design balance, the pool house mirrors the bedroom wing in its wood plank construction in and out. We created this little house to have a dedicated indoor-outdoor space near the pool, but we use it just as much for guests. With kids now frequently visiting, we made a pair of bedrooms here—one with a trim, built-in bunk and trundle bed. It may be the smallest bedroom we've ever done, almost nautical in style for this compact space, but everything fits and tucks away perfectly.

Opposite A stone gym is set within the shelter of several old heritage oaks at the edge of the pool and the garden. Large agave and other native, drought-tolerant plants populate the garden in an extension of the local terrain.

Following The front façade of the main house is shaded by newly planted, mature olive trees. The two stonework volumes of the building, the great room and the billiard room, are connected by a breezeway-like entry hall. We discovered huge deposits of Santa Barbara sandstone when we dug all the foundations on the property—a surprise that helped inspire the composition of the house and supplied us with our own material.

Overleaf (left) A view over the lawn from the main house. Some of the excavated rocks were left for character and accents among the plantings. **(right)** The entry hall is most often left open during long stays. Stone walls wrap into the corridor to create the impression of being between buildings.

Previous The great room brings together the kitchen, dining area, and living room in one central space that we use constantly. The garden-facing wall of this room opens via thirty-foot-wide floor-to-ceiling, sliding, steel-and-glass doors. A broad deck is part of the living experience year-round, with the tableaux of the mountains and the garden visible from inside, and lounging and dining extending outside through the seasons.

Opposite Bleached knotty oak floors, beamed cedar ceilings, and integral color plaster walls create the natural palette for the kitchen. As this is a vacation home, we didn't need to be slaves to the practical, so we decided to do away with upper cabinets. French Blue De Savoie marble covers counters and the backsplash behind the range. Three vintage milk glass pendant lights unify the sections of the room.

Above The sitting area in the great room is presided over by a towering fireplace made from our Santa Barbara sandstone. The sofa and pair of vintage chairs are upholstered in easy fabrics.

Previous Views to the mountains encircle the property. The main living spaces occupy the stone structures; the bedrooms are in the cedar plank wing to the right. The pool house in the foreground mirrors the bedroom wing.

Above A restored 1950s bronze and walnut pool table is the centerpiece of the billiard room.

Opposite A glass passageway floats between the stone buildings and the wood-clad bedroom wing, becoming both a transparency and a sculpture outside of the house.

Previous The master suite is located at the secluded end of the bedroom wing, near the kitchen garden where the plantings become more wild and natural. The long, custom parchment cabinet accommodates storage and art.

Opposite The recessed shower serves as an open picture window onto a private green wall of the garden.

Above Vintage brass sconces and lacquered brass hardware add a golden glow to the master bathroom. The nine-foot-long reeded walnut washstand was inspired by 1950s Italian cabinets.

Previous The pool house is equipped for both recreation and as a guesthouse with an additional two bedrooms. The space provides proximity to shade and amenities during the day, including a bathroom, a changing room, and a small kitchen.

Above We designed the pool house with the qualities of an open-air living space. Pocketing doors connect a breezy central sitting room to the pool deck. Indiana limestone paving continues from outside to inside.

Opposite The composition of the fireplace in the pool house is particularly beautiful. All the fireplaces on the property were traditionally hand-pieced by an expert mason. Vintage chairs and a custom sofa give the space versatility for indoor-outdoor use.

Opposite The fully detailed and fitted bunk room is one of our favorites; yet, it's the smallest bedroom we've ever done. Each bunk has its own window and shutter. A trundle below adds another bed for sleepovers.

Above (left) Durably designed for lots of activity, yet gracious for guests, the bathroom at the pool house has walls clad in natural quartzite stone and the continuous limestone flooring used throughout the structure. **(right)** A high-walled outdoor shower by the stone gym is a favorite that's used year-round.

Following The house at dusk. Year-round, it's lovely to be outside here as the light changes. The outdoor fireplace off the billiard room is a favorite spot for s'mores.

BEVERLY HILLS

This commission began as a grand vacation house for a large family from overseas. A sophisticated European businessman and his elegant wife wanted a home base in Beverly Hills for summers and holidays in the United States. Rather than follow the typical migration to the countryside for a holiday home, this gave us a chance to think of Beverly Hills as an international destination in and of itself for global citizens. The fun of it was the client's very fashionable, vanguard style, which gave us an invitation to think quite outside of the box in terms of the entire design, from the architecture to the grounds to the interiors. The home is ultimately more extravagant, visually and materially, than my usual approach to modernism. But it has a lot of the same easy California soul that I try to bring to all my projects.

The assignment was to replace an older, smaller, vintage house on the property they'd found with a striking, modern residence. The priority was to include a range of open-air spaces for the family's orientation to outdoor living and their great pleasure in entertaining. We were also asked to provide multiple guest quarters to accommodate family and friends coming abroad for extended summer visits. Our concept was to compose the house out of a series of public and private pavilions. We approached the design in the spirit of a boutique hotel, with separate yet related spaces for varied groups, and some of the movie star glamour of a Riviera villa.

In the resulting layout, the ground floor of the main house holds the living room, dining room, and family room in a long row, all designed for stylish hosting. These rooms open onto generous, covered lanai-style patios for spending time outside in the shade.

The upper level of the house is primarily assigned for the kids. Moving to the large, sheltered backyard, a glazed breezeway connects to a master suite located in its own surrounding reflecting pool. A guest house at the far end of the yard includes more bedrooms upstairs, with a covered outdoor room flanked by a full spa and gym downstairs. And all this circulates around an enormous, turquoise-water, hotel-sized pool.

The exterior cladding of the house became an important design element to solve for crucial privacy from the street. We wrapped the second story of the building in a curving, horizontal aluminum grillage that creates ribs of light and shadow as the sun moves around the property.

Bringing this dappled light inside, we incorporated ornamental finishes that are devoted to sparkle and texture. Mirror is a frequent material, used with a deco spirit. The lady of the house's favored shades of pink, lavender, silver, and pale blue inform not only the décor and the custom furnishings we made, but also architectural elements like a set of frosted glass panels in the long front hallway. These colors softly deepen as the light changes with the day, letting the whole house feel like the glow of a sunrise or sunset, more jeweled and chic than casual and beachy.

Opposite A curving marble staircase is the glamorous centerpiece of the entry hall. Undulating, rounded shapes recur throughout the house in both the architecture and décor, creating a sense of fluidity. Here and elsewhere, lustrous silk carpets are inset to be perfectly flush with the terrazzo floors. Walls of striated and lacquered wood paneling create glossy patterns of reflection that echo the grillage outside. A glass breezeway floats over a reflecting pool, connecting the master bedroom wing to the main house.

Following (left) The front of the house is set behind a curved driveway. A painted aluminum, louvered grillage surrounds the second floor, creating a protective screen from the sun and the street. Translucent glass panels on the first floor further veil the house on the exterior, while admitting softly colored light inside. **(right)** The back stair wraps around a glass-enclosed elevator that connects the basement, first, and second floors.

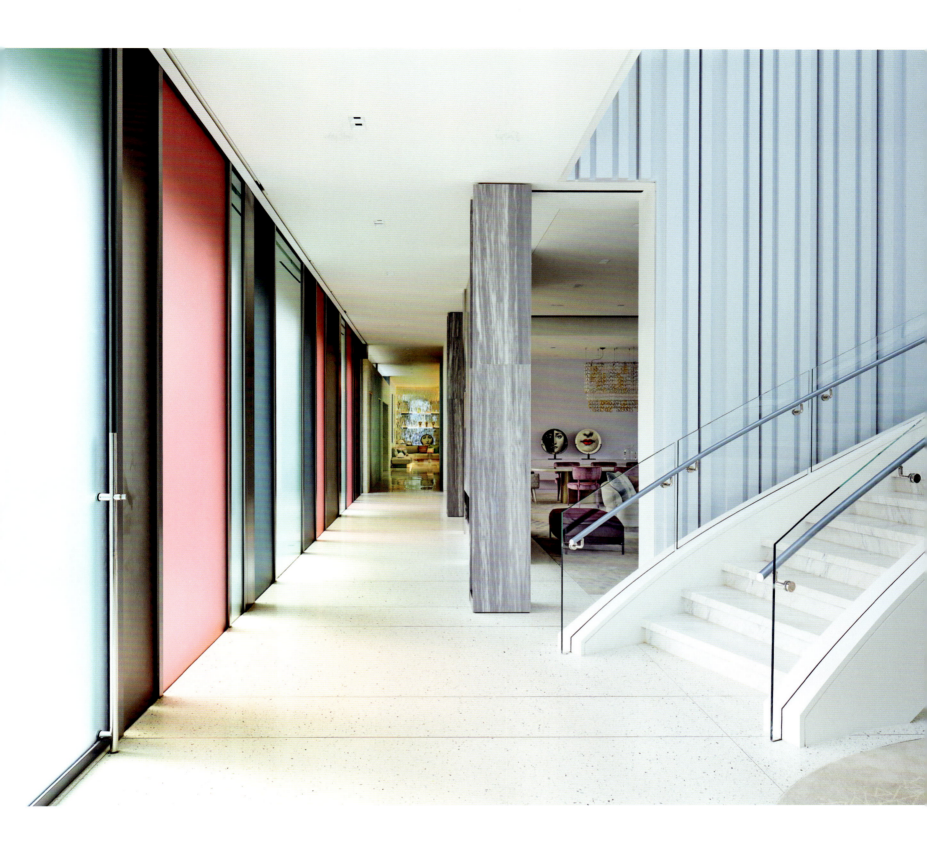

Opposite The colored glass panels in the front hallway cast a pearly light that changes in intensity over the course of the day. Echoing these shades, the interiors feature gem-like aquas, pinks, and burnished metals that reverberate against the white spaces.

Above A long, open hallway connects the family areas on the main floor. Frosted and colored glass panels cast tinted shadows onto the floors. Throughout the house, custom terrazzo incorporates bits of mirror, shell, and marble for shine. The prominent columns around the living space are made of Turkish marble.

Following The living room and dining room form one salon-like space. For full indoor-outdoor living and frequent hosting, this room opens onto a large terrace that includes bar, eating, and lounging areas. The guesthouse and pool are visible beyond in the vast backyard. The site plan was inspired by the idea of a boutique hotel, so as to provide leisure spaces and accommodations for the family's many guests and visitors.

Previous In the dining room area, Fornasetti objects are displayed on a custom-designed table with a rippling, golden brass base. More of the collection tops the companion lacquer and glass buffet cabinet. The chandelier is made of glass chain links in clear, gold, and silver leaf finishes. The pink dining chairs are faux-shagreen-textured velvet.

Opposite (clockwise from top left) A demilune backrest accentuates the sensual shape of a fully upholstered custom dining chair. The long, stretched arc of the stairway is silhouetted against a wall of sculpted wood panels. The dining room's floating buffet cabinet was designed by Kazuko. The oval kitchen island is made with a lacquered and reeded base and topped with blue onyx.

Above In the family room, a cantilevered banquette provides extra seating. More Fornasetti and colorful objects float on clear Plexiglas shelves in front of a mirror-mosaic wall.

Following The family room has a simple kitchen with a breakfast bar alcove tucked behind an opening in the limestone wall beyond. A full chef's kitchen is located between this space and the dining room.

Opposite The breakfast table looks out toward the master bedroom pavilion. Mod bucket chairs and a banquette for extra seating add to the wave-like motif of the décor.

Above The door to the powder room is made with inlaid leather panels and structural chrome hardware, juxtaposed against the texture of a split limestone wall. The powder room itself is enclosed by grasscloth walls that have a subtle, graphite sheen, surrounding a minimalist, carved block sink of Italian marble.

Following (left) The back wall of the entry hall opens onto a reflecting pool; the extending glass breezeway links the main house to the master suite. The retractable louvered grille over the second floor wraps the house in an ever-changing pattern of shadows, while providing enclosure for the kids' rooms upstairs. **(right)** The passage to the master suite looks into a sitting room, centered on a modern, sculptural, custom tufted sofa.

Previous The master bedroom is surrounded by a lily pond for privacy and serenity. We intended this wing to be a Zen-like retreat for the couple, with the feel of a pavilion suspended in its own reflecting pool. A promontory-like patio sits over the main water, absorbing the morning sun.

Above The ladies' bath features a wall of vertical glass and mirror mosaic. The tiling creates waves of dappled light, shimmering around the teacup-shaped tub. A mirrored backdrop multiplies the depth of the room in a classic Hollywood style, backing a custom-designed vanity and a pair of vintage Italian sconces.

Opposite A Venetian crystal chandelier adds classic luxury to the modernism of the master bedroom. The walls are clad in a plaster-based covering that gives the room a natural marbled texture. Back-painted glass and elongated panels of silk upholstery form the headboard. Silk carpet adds to the luminous envelope.

Following and overleaf The property afforded space for a pool that would be central entertaining, and hotel-like in scale. An additional track of the pool wraps around the outdoor lounge to create an eighty-two-foot-long lap lane, for more-serious swimmers. For the pool, we chose a hexagonal glass tile in varied aquatic gradations that amplify the movement and depth of color in the water as it changes throughout the day.

CANYON FARMHOUSE

The setting of a west-side canyon brought together the best of two worlds—country and city—in the design of this family home. This location allowed a creative couple with young kids to reinvent an idea of sophisticated farmhouse living close to town, without giving up a connection to nature day to day.

The main challenge of the project was its site planning. The lot was set within a scenic woodland in the canyon, but it was quite oddly shaped, like the outline of a cowhide. I needed to put a rectilinear house inside of an irregular shape, and, in doing so, disguise the uneven perimeter of the land. At the same time, it was critical to maximize as much of the property as I could for outdoor living.

The couple had initially asked for a big family backyard. That would typically mean pushing a house to one edge of a lot. But doing this didn't get the house to open to the outdoors in a liberal way. What worked best was to position the house in the middle of the lot; and though this made for a shallower backyard, it gave us instead three different outdoor areas that would enhance more of the family's activities.

These three areas are really outdoor rooms. They dictate the layout of the house and help to locate the views. We used the shelter of one immovable, heritage live oak tree to create shade for the living room and the husband's office. A wide gravel courtyard around the tree is set up for large-scale evening entertaining, with a long outdoor dining table and a firepit. On the east side of the house, we made a secluded, walled seating area, anchored by a big, outdoor stone fireplace, as a social extension of the dining room. The sunniest southern part of the property was reserved for the pool area and traditional backyard, opening naturally off the kitchen and breakfast room, with a covered terrace.

For design reference, we all agreed stylistically on an updated farmhouse, made primarily in wood—our city version of a Canyon House. I was drawn to box mouldings and coffered paneling, wainscoting, picture rails, beams, and casings that allude to classic nineteenth-century cottage architecture. Then we enlarged all the proportions and brought the mouldings down to simple, flat profiles, so that they would create attention without feeling heavy or too formal in the rooms. These honest details also help to bring down the scale of the house's tall, large spaces.

Finish and color were just as important to the craft of the house as the woodwork. The idea was to give each of the principal rooms its own identity, in a continuum of light and dark spaces. Paint colors and wood stains are velvety and soft in tone. They catch the light with a warm patina. All these gestures place the architecture in a more American, New England tradition than a European one. And they give the new house an aura of history that feels well-lived in, even now.

Opposite The entrance to the house faces a secluded cul-de-sac. The high volume of the stair hall is seen framed through the steel-framed picture window at the front door.

Above Updating a Canyon House idiom, the airy front entrance is positioned on a slight rise and sheltered under a long porch. The exterior walls are clad in Santa Barbara sandstone, along with painted wood siding and beams; the stairs and paving are made of Indiana limestone. The porch provides an additional layer of privacy between the entry and the curb.

Opposite The wood and bronze stairway climbs the corner of the entry hall. Classic box paneling allowed us to break up the walls and mediate the scale of this two-story, light-filled space; the paneling travels upward to become the wainscot in all the hallways on the second floor. This millwork brings a softer, historical American gesture to the house, but at this enlarged scale it feels pleasantly simple and unfussy.

Following The family room has a beamed, cathedral ceiling and box moulding along the fireplace wall, continuing the use of farmhouse and cottage architectural details at this new, enlarged scale. We deliberately kept the second story off this portion of the house so that we could have more volume in this much-used room. With both southern and western exposures, it has beautiful light all day.

Right: Rather than create one unbroken great room for this house, the family room is connected to the kitchen and breakfast area through a wide, cased opening. In the kitchen, box paneling adds interest to the ceiling, echoing the fireplace wall in the next room. All the cabinetry here makes use of honest, framed details and applied mouldings that come out of the same traditional American millwork exercise as the wall and ceiling paneling.

Previous The kitchen is characterized by warm materials and finishes in ranges of cream rather than bright modern white. The goal across the house was to convey a subtle vintage and country feeling without looking rustic. The island is cerused white oak; the wood cabinets are painted a gentle putty color. The hood above the range is plaster. Pale marble countertops are used throughout. Brass sabot feet complete a number of the cabinetry pieces in the house; in the kitchen, all the brass fittings and faucets are left unlacquered to patina over time.

Above The breakfast area off the kitchen is positioned by a large, sunny wall of windows, with a vista that includes the backyard and pool. A covered porch echoes the simple colonnaded form along the front entrance of the house.

Opposite The kids' craft room, appointed with vintage furniture, opens directly to the outside. We created this room to provide a flexible space that the couple would evolve over time with the children, as they grow and their needs change.

Previous The office features one of the house's darker interiors, juxtaposed with a bright, natural exterior. The objective was to create a secluded working space that would have a refined seriousness about it. Adding intrigue, this hidden room is accessed through a blind door in the living room. With the space facing north and east, we gave it two high glass-and-steel exterior walls to let it feel as if it's directly in the garden. The other two walls are ebonized oak, evoking a masculine, country house study.

Opposite The dining room courtyard is especially inviting at nighttime, in the glow of a fireplace amid the greenery and trees. The hearth and the walls of the courtyard are clad in one continuous expanse of hand-fitted pieces of Santa Barbara sandstone.

Above The dining room is given a singular identity with a rich, dark charcoal paint finish over elegant paneling. The room connects to one of the outdoor spaces that we created, inviting diners to go in and outside freely during gatherings.

Following The living room is arranged in the spirit of a salon. The house is furnished throughout with a mix of special vintage modern and antique pieces collected by the owner, notably from Scandinavia, the Netherlands, and Belgium. This space opens to, and is designed to be a part of, the primary courtyard for outdoor entertaining.

Previous Connection and privacy. **(left)** The high, open volume of the entry hall was chosen so as to connect the second floor to the goings-on below. The idea was that people shouldn't be isolated when they're upstairs; the whole family can communicate. **(right)** At the same time, we wanted to make room for the unique work routines of the owners, adding a quiet library to the master bedroom, along with the main office downstairs, to accommodate concentration during their different work hours.

Above The master bathroom is given a sophisticated boost with slabs of dramatically figured linear marble, cut to form a wide chevron pattern. The classic, appointed cabinetry is painted a soft, flattering grey, and configured in a his-and-hers layout. The tub sits in a central alcove with the best long view down the canyon.

Opposite The master bedroom and its peaceful deck are positioned to enjoy the lovely southern treetop views of the canyon. This space, like the family room downstairs, gains loft and light and a canyon aesthetic with its vaulted and beamed ceiling.

Following The back of the house, with its many old-growth trees silhouetted in the twilight, faces the third outdoor space: a traditional family backyard with the pool. The pool is aligned with the outdoor eating area. Covered seating by the kitchen provides shade during the day, and heat and light during the evening, to maximize the use of the outdoors.

WILSHIRE

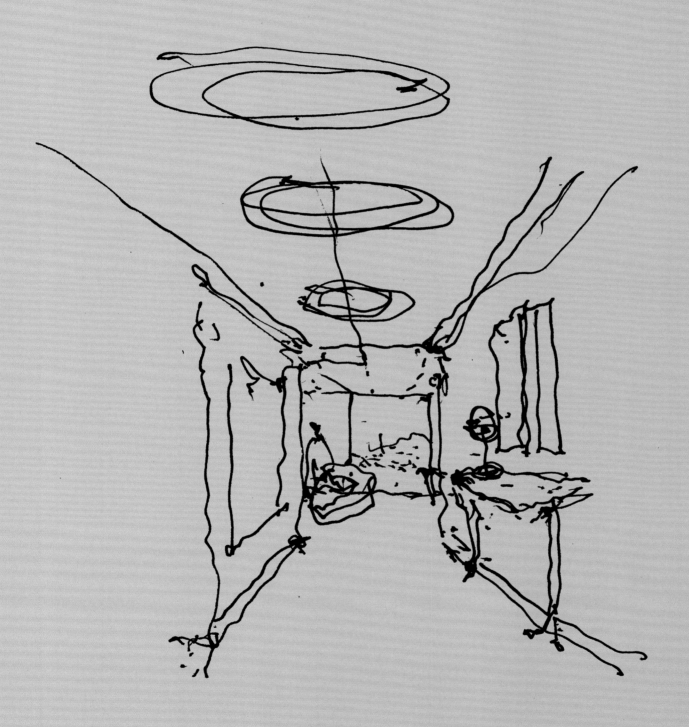

I've always felt that a California home doesn't have to be just a house on the ground. It can be a place up in the sky, a gorgeous apartment. In the case of apartment living, one of the special things you can gain is elevation, often with cinemascope views that aren't attainable any other way.

I love the traditions of apartment living in other cities. In Los Angeles we have a long history of beautiful art deco and postwar architecture in grand apartment buildings and hotels from the 1930s onward. So I stepped into this project of redesigning a collector's art-filled condo with plenty of inspiration. For a client who travels frequently, keeping and updating her current, spacious flat made sense—letting her come and go with ease and minimal maintenance. The notion was to create a tranquil retreat in the style of a sophisticated Parisian or Roman *pied-à-terre*, and to make sure the spaces were an inviting background to the art.

The apartment occupies a high, bright floor in a newer modern building. We were charged with reimagining the existing plan and giving the space a fresh, completely bespoke fabrication. Throughout, the primary gesture was one of subtraction, stripping back prior ornamentation in favor of refined simplicity with exceptional proportions, opulent materials, and a mix of surfaces to cast and catch light throughout the space, day and night.

An important choice early on was to create built-in, lacquered cabinetry in the kitchen, bathroom, and office. Practical yet a little dressy, the cabinets bring both reflection and a shared vocabulary of pared-down paneling to the whole residence, while providing a surprising amount of organized storage. In all the rooms, minimalistic details like flush doors, wide hallways, no mouldings, and spare downlighting give the space a sense of quietness and air. Large soffits, drapery to the ceiling, and the naturally stepped configuration of the perimeter walls help to visually divide the open living area from the kitchen, creating an alcove for a diminutive breakfast booth, another for a dining area, yet allowing all the zones to feel connected. While the architecture is very linear, the rooms seem to float and feel organic, punctuated with colorful works and expanded by the wide, windowed vistas and balconies that look over the city all the way to the ocean.

The owner's modern personal style guided the equilibrium of the interiors. We wanted the furnishings and palette to convey softness and femininity with an *au courant* confidence. A selective use of atmospheric neutrals and visually tactile materials produces a warm, luxurious envelope, as though suspended in the clouds—smoothly plastered walls and shades of pale periwinkle, gentle grey, and blush; bleached-oak plank floors; plush silk and wool carpets that buffer sound. Instead of more maximal layers, simple juxtaposition is used to create dimension, with solid expanses of special Bardiglio Nuvolato marble and silvery travertine against all the delicate, glossy cabinetry. Throughout, the furniture is carefully curated and uncluttered, a mix of vintage collectible pieces and contemporary designs. Large, sculptural, curvilinear furnishings with soft edges add to a feeling of cushioned, comfortable elegance that's inviting to sink into. With a minimum number of objects to fill the eye, the attention goes to the art, the senses, and beyond, to the views.

Opposite Entering the apartment from its own private elevator, the main hallway proceeds toward the open living area and the view beyond to the ocean. Because this residence is on a higher floor with very bright south and west exposures, we used a soft, cocooning grey for the walls and whitewashed oak floors throughout to warm the space. The blue, lacquered console was chosen specifically to hold pieces from the client's art collection.

Previous The living room is anchored by a custom, very comfortable, curving sectional sofa. As this seating area is central, we wanted to make sure the shape looked beautiful and inviting from every angle. Kazuko designed the reeded oak armoire as a more linear, geometric counterpoint for additional storage between the living and dining areas.

Opposite We worked to customize the seemingly freehand pattern of the living room's silk rug, playing with negative space and scale so that the linework dances in a very intentional way, and is laid out with respect to where all the furniture is placed.

Above A custom bar cabinet with a built-in wine cooler is made of back-painted glass panels in a matte, bronze finish, and topped with marble. Above it, an artwork from the client's collection is backlit so that the picture glows.

Following (left) A game table area is tucked into one corner of the living room, with a custom oak table and a banquette designed to let people angle in comfortably. A very large fireplace mantel made of striated Platinum marble meets the scale of the paired artworks that we knew would be placed on either side. **(right)** The dining area makes use of a natural alcove in the floor plan. The table is made of back-painted glass and the unusual light fixtures were specially installed to be interlocking, as a form of sculpture.

Previous The kitchen flows into the dining area in a harmonized palette of soothing, light blue and grey tones, and rich materials. The open floor plan demanded solutions that would keep the whole space feeling seamless and integrated. Neat, built-in cabinets in the window bays hold storage, as does all the sleekly paneled, uncluttered cabinetry in the kitchen.

Opposite To accommodate the client's wish for a breakfast nook, we created a small, built-in banquette for two, raised slightly on a platform so the seats could be at window level. This is a lovely spot in the soft morning light from which to enjoy the view west to the beach. Lavender Ultrasuede on the banquettes adds a layer of fresh, more saturated blue to the space.

Above The kitchen is made with a system of high-gloss lacquer cabinets that create ample storage while reducing the busy look of all the appliances. Wonderful slabs of Bardiglio Nuvolato marble cover a full backsplash wall as well as the countertops. Bronzed glass panels add translucency to a bay of upper cabinets; the Oro Puro waterfall bar counter provides a clean transition into the dining area.

Previous The master bedroom began with the design of the modern, subtly winged bed frame. We also decided to graduate from the blues of the living space into a rosier, warmer taupe palette that would feel very restful for the client. All the furniture is custom and upholstered in fine, soft fabrics. The special wall covering is hand-painted to look like dimensional plaster.

Opposite In the sitting area of the master suite, biomorphic glass sconces hang on either side of a cabinet that holds a television. These unique pieces felt like wall sculptures to complement the client's art collection, and they glow beautifully when lit. The plush wool carpet provides a luxurious, cushioned footfall with an integrated wave pattern of pile to cut loop.

Above Spare, clean planes and lavish materials carry over to the master bath from the rest of the residence. Particularly thick, large format slabs of Taj Mahal-marble clad much of the environment without feeling heavy. Following the lacquer cabinetry in the kitchen, the vanity and a built-in vitrine are handled in a slightly warmer grey finish; shelves are lit from inside. Behind one mirror is a medicine cabinet; the other holds a television that ingeniously transmits through the glass.

NEW LONDON

The spirit of this house is more English than some of our other projects. On trips to London, I'd often admired the way that refined, period Georgian buildings were being renovated inside with very modern, crisp white, luxuriously simple interiors. That juxtaposition appealed to this client, a couple with a young family, who had outgrown a traditional Cape Cod house and were ready to build something new from the ground up. They wanted a house that would blend into their neighborhood, in a distinguished old section of Beverly Hills. But they'd also grown committed to modern design as their tastes progressed. The solution was a home that is not so much contemporary as it is a radical distillation of an earlier, classically English set of forms.

It always strikes me to think of how fresh the architecture of Sir John Soane and the Adam Brothers must have seemed in the eighteenth century, and why modern interiors live so well inside those neoclassical spaces. For this project, I wanted to take that feeling to the next level. Accordingly, the house follows a tranquil, symmetrical Georgian plan, with tall and elegant proportions. It faces the street in a classical way, like the older houses around it. In the English style, I chose painted white brick, but then paired it with steel windows instead of wood to bring in a later modernism.

The interior is built around a two-story atrium. With a floor plan of this considerable size, we wanted to avoid the central areas of the house becoming dark. To brighten the core, the entry hall was made as a double volume illuminated by a large, elliptical skylight. A floating, curved stair borrows from the slender shaping of staircases in older London townhouses. This form unfolds in one continuous, graceful sweep to the upstairs hallway. The airiness and natural light in this space, up and down, assure that it's never dark inside, anywhere. The hall functions almost like an interior courtyard.

In this same spirit of reinventing a traditional house, the living room and dining room are formally paired, opening off the central hall. Both rooms have fireplaces and exactly the same pattern of windows. The walls have layered plaster details that are suggestive of paneling, so that the spaces have a cadence. All the cabinetry and stonework in the kitchen, bathrooms, and dressing rooms express dramatically simple geometry. These features recall the floating white rooms that I've so enjoyed in London, very light and elevated and wonderfully proportioned, within a classical shell. But here, with all the openness and the many windows, the house also draws in the different warmth of the California light.

The minimalism does not mean that these rooms are plain. Spare and cool as the architecture may seem, the house is designed to be calming. There is an absoluteness of form in beautiful finishes that allowed us to create a feeling of completeness, with spaces very balanced at their essence, even before the house was decorated.

Opposite A painted brick exterior, carved limestone pediment, and steel casement windows lend a deliberately classical look to the front façade of the house.

Following The house faces the street with a simple yet formal structure. The symmetry and proportions are reinforced by the gentle order of the plantings. Branching olive trees provide airy looseness for balance.

Above The stair hall with its curving upper gallery is at once minimal and classical. Simplified details derived from nineteenth-century English architecture establish the character of the stairway and the interior at large.

Opposite The view through the hall is uninterrupted from the front entry all the way outside to the rear of the property, terminating beyond the pool on a focal sculptural element. Limestone flooring creates a subtle pattern through the use of two textures: polished and honed.

Above The dining room has a fireplace that matches the living room. The minimally stepped paneling around the entry echoes fine mouldings with a much simplified effect, following the theme of distilled classical detail throughout the house.

Opposite Strict symmetry was followed throughout the design of all the formal rooms, though the spaces also have a lightness that brings them a lofty ease. As seen in the living room, careful layers of built-up plaster create a panelized effect in the place of traditional moulding. The lighting and other structures such as drapery hardware are organized in deep, recessed grooves in the ceiling, creating the effect that the rooms seem to float within the walls.

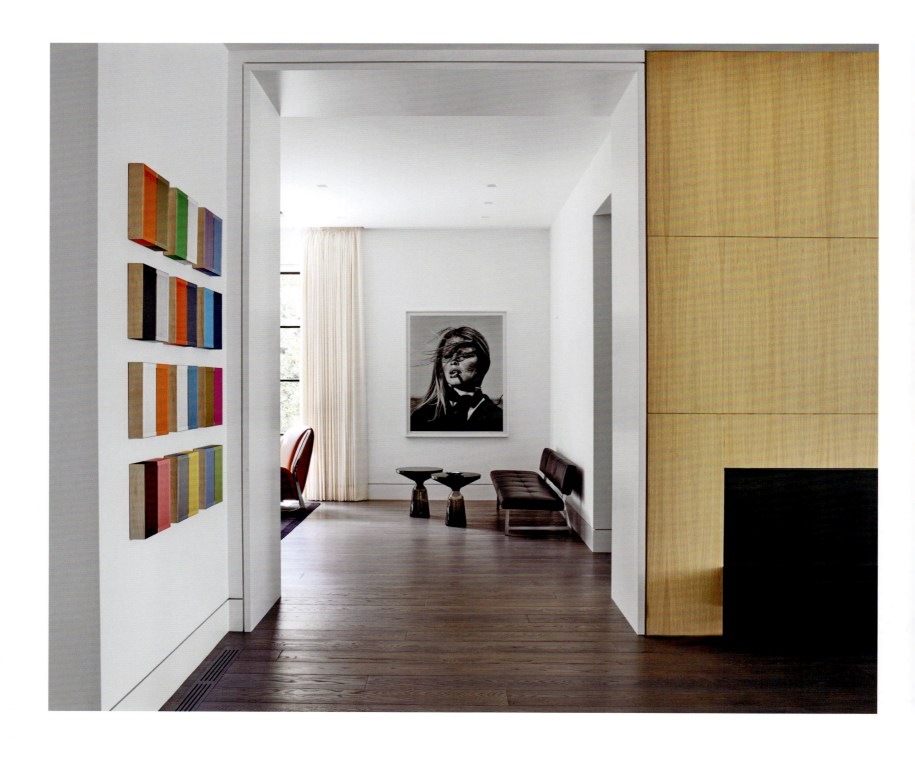

Previous The family room unfolds on the central axis of the house, situated between the entry hall and the backyard. Embracing the large, open scale in the back area of the plan, this much-used space flows into the kitchen in one loft-like great room configuration.

Above A hall off the family room provides entry to the gentlemen's area, which includes the husband's office, a wine room, and a bar. Greyed oak floors and warm, rift-cut white oak paneling—carried over from the fireplace wall—create the palette for this interior. The mood is less the pure, spare white envelope of the formal spaces, more late 1940s clubroom in inspiration.

Above Visible through a glass wall, the wine room is designed as an extension of the bar room and is clad in unfinished oak. The shelving is built to accommodate the storage and display of a collection of oversized bottles. The French doors lead to a private terrace for cigar smoking.

Following The great room is deliberately oversized so as to create more definitive separation between the dining area, the kitchen, and the family room seating. For all its simplicity, the spaciousness feels luxurious.

Previous The adjacent kitchen is very functional yet innately streamlined. Sleek kitchen cabinets of anodized metal and stainless steel, a wall of windows in lieu of upper shelving, and minimized kitchen appliances reduce the working image of the space. An adjacent sous kitchen allows for this simplicity. Built-in storage behind a clean grid of drawers and cupboards allows for seamless concealment of the kitchen equipment. The cooktop is set flush into the countertop, maintaining the elegant spareness of the Bianca marble countertops, as does the sink in the stainless-steel island.

Opposite A covered porch connects directly to the dining area, through French doors that breezily stay open much of the time.

Above The family room opens fully to the backyard terrace through pocketing doors. Raised decks accommodate sun lounging and a firepit on either side of the pool. The slightly elevated grade of the pool creates a stepped landscape that increases interest and a sense of depth in the backyard.

Following Behind the firepit, a garage with steel-and-glass doors provides display for special autos. The space is intentionally presented as an artful part of the outdoor experience. Next to this sitting area, the zero-edge pool is fully surfaced both inside and out in an especially beautiful shade of turquoise glass tile, which is revealed as the pool rim steps down to the lawn.

Previous (left) The powder room is a study in elongated proportions, like the narrow, very tall doors and windows throughout the house. A crystallized blue-grey marble block is suspended as a floating sink in front of a textured wall, keeping the palette light. **(right)** Equally handsome in stone and just as abstractly sculptural, the stairs are made with extra-deep, inch-and-a-half-thick limestone treads.

Opposite A very large, oculus skylight with a steel-and-glass diffuser echoes the curving oval of the stair. The skylight ensures that the center of the house, and all upstairs circulation areas, are bright during the day. The spacious gallery at the top of the stairs provides long walls for artwork.

Following The lady's office is upstairs, with a view of the backyard and pool. Rich lacquer paneling is crafted with the same spare detailing as the gentleman's oak-paneled office and the formal rooms downstairs, but here to the effect of enveloping the space in a deep, glowing lapis blue.

Previous Very spare but not austere, the master bedroom is luxurious with light and open space. A sculptural wall of custom-designed paneling with integral nightstands, and the bed frame, are made in the same rift-cut white oak that appears in other parts of the house. A television is stored in the chest at the foot of the bed.

Above Each fixture in the master bath is a different primary shape, likened to a form of sculpture. The effort was to make the room as essential and open as possible, letting in the view of the backyard, especially for soaks in the seamless egg-shaped tub.

Opposite Cantilevering off the wall, a pair of Pullman cabinets takes the form of symmetrical sink vanities. The cabinetry is made of oak, cased in a floating frame of inch-and-a-quarter-thick marble. The mirrors are designed to be inset flush into the wall, so as to not interrupt the planes of the room.

Following The closets in the master suite are entirely clad in rift-cut oak and separated into two sections for the husband and wife. The glass-enclosed shoe 'pantry' was specifically designed to store shoes and bags in a dust-free environment.

Overleaf The back of the house, aglow in the evening. The building is precisely aligned to reflect in the blue pool. While this rear façade leans in a more contemporary direction, it still maintains the symmetrical, stately character of the front.

PALISADES RANCH

The inspiration for this project was to rethink a classic ranch house in a refined modern vernacular. Starting with a sunny, flat lot in Pacific Palisades, I envisioned a home that would combine the original ranch heritage of this region with a more contemporary, open, two-story layout. The exterior did need to fit the character of a vintage neighborhood with older houses. At the same time, the client, a couple, was inclined to a modern interior, in part to suit their art collection. Most of all, they wanted a home that would be abundantly filled with natural light.

Following tradition, the main living spaces are built in a C-shape around an inner courtyard. Most of the rooms have windows on three sides, offering views to all parts of the property. We sequenced the house on an east–west line, so that each room fills with sun over the course of the day. This lets the clients enjoy every space at its optimal point, from first to last light.

To balance light with shade, we gave the front façade a long, open-air porch with slender columns. The porch and colonnade invoke iconic ranch style and help to layer the view of the house from the street. Old-growth olive trees were brought into the front garden to create a more-established landscape, letting the house feel as if it's been there for some time.

For building materials, we chose a combination of traditional painted wood siding and ivory Texas limestone; this stone in particular because it splits so nicely, and because of its soft, mottled color. Both in and out, the architecture is distilled down to just a few elemental materials, but it's not remote. The understatement is highly crafted and quite tactile, embodying a spare American elegance.

Inside, the house is subtle and modern in detail. The floating stairway is unembellished, formed with stained oak and a glass railing. We used this mellow oak throughout to add grounding and warmth to the very light, airy rooms. The dining room, master bedroom, family room, and den are each anchored by a wall of oak paneling to the same effect. Generous, flat-front wood cabinetry adds to the feeling, enriching the light colors and finishes around it without seeming vintage.

The rear section of the house opens with views onto a secluded, sunlit backyard, from both the main floor and the master suite upstairs. A covered patio off the family room and kitchen includes a fireplace and lighted seating as well as a dining area; it's become a favorite outdoor room that the couple uses for much of their entertaining. From this position, the pool sits slightly above the lawn in a field of tone-on-tone green plantings, yielding a richness of color around the house without introducing any additional colors or flowers. We intentionally placed the pool here along the perimeter of the yard as the point of last light for the house. Raised up just this small amount, it can be appreciated from the rooms inside, the water shimmering at the end of the day.

Opposite The double-height entry hall features a floating stairway made of rift-cut oak with glass rails. The pared-down geometry of the form sets the tone for the modern-leaning interior. The center table is by Ron Chad.

Following The house is clad in split-face Texas limestone on the first story and painted wood siding on the second floor. Standing seam zinc completes the envelope. The colonnaded porch shelters the front rooms from the sun in classic ranch house style.

Overleaf Four old-growth olive trees frame a quiet seating area next to the house. The trees were sourced from vintage olive groves north of Los Angeles; each one was selected for its sculptural qualities.

Previous In the living room, a split-face limestone fireplace rises fifteen feet to the cathedral ceiling. Refined, painted wood beams add detail to the ceiling while remaining crisp and modern.

Opposite The courtyard is shared by the dining room, living room, and family room. The custom steel doors and windows fall in the parts of the home that are stone clad; wooden window casings are in the wood portions of the house. These windows share the same tall size around the wings of the courtyard, so that the different sections of the house feel equal.

Following Pocketing glass doors allow the dining room to open fully to the courtyard. A custom tiered fountain is gracious in tradition but modern in design.

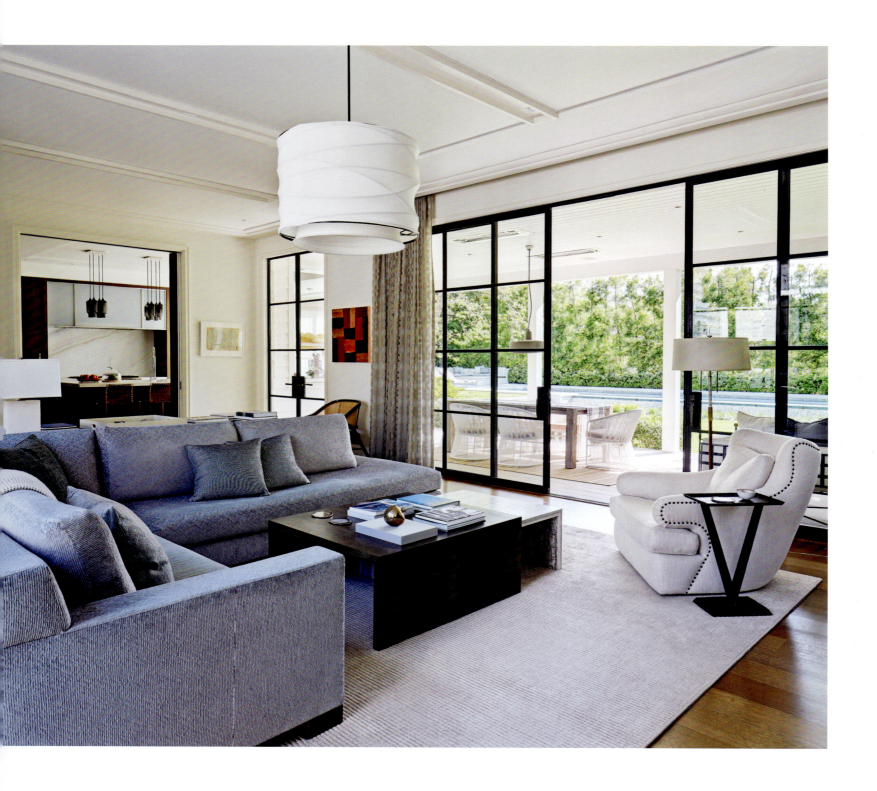

Above Extending from the kitchen, the family room opens to the covered back patio by means of sliding steel-and-glass windows. The long lap pool forms a third stage of these connected spaces, merging lengthwise with the lawn.

Opposite The kitchen enjoys the morning sun with a built-in breakfast space along a wide bay window. The room opens onto the backyard for indoor-outdoor living. All the cabinetry throughout the house is made in the same rift-cut oak, elevating a feeling of simplicity.

Following Slabs of simply paneled oak clad an entire wall, adding warmth to the study. The room was located so that it would be lit by afternoon sun, at the time of day when the owners commonly use it.

Overleaf The entry hall is anchored by a custom wall of blue-grey back-painted glass, providing a soft color field in contrast with the wooden stairway.

Previous The master suite includes a glass-balconied patio that overlooks the backyard. This generous outdoor space makes the bedroom feel enveloped and hotel-like. As in other rooms, a wall of rift-cut oak provides a warm visual anchor. We used it here to create a background for the bed. The custom louvers are also made in oak.

Above (left) Across from the bed, a custom-built media wall echoes the simple lines and fine woodwork of all the cabinetry in the house. **(right)** In the master bathroom, we created a central floor motif of intersecting, soft-cornered squares of inlaid marble, which appears like a stone area rug. Our craftsmen inset the slender pattern so that it is seamless within the marble floor. A coved skylight over the sinks adds natural light where it's needed.

Opposite The large bathroom extends the thematic lightness of the house, with an open floor plan and sun pouring in through a wall of windows. A cabinet wall incorporates the lady's vanity, all made in the house's simply paneled rift oak. The tub is elevated one step up on a platform to take advantage of the view onto the backyard.

Following The covered patio in the backyard provides an extended seating and dining area for outdoor entertaining. In order to keep the space functional into the evening, we added interior-style fixture lighting. The outdoor fireplace is clad in split-face limestone for consistency and visual effect.

Overleaf As the outdoor component of the family room, the patio has become the most popular location in the house—a restful destination at the end of the day for the owners, and the place for much of their entertaining.

HOT SPRINGS

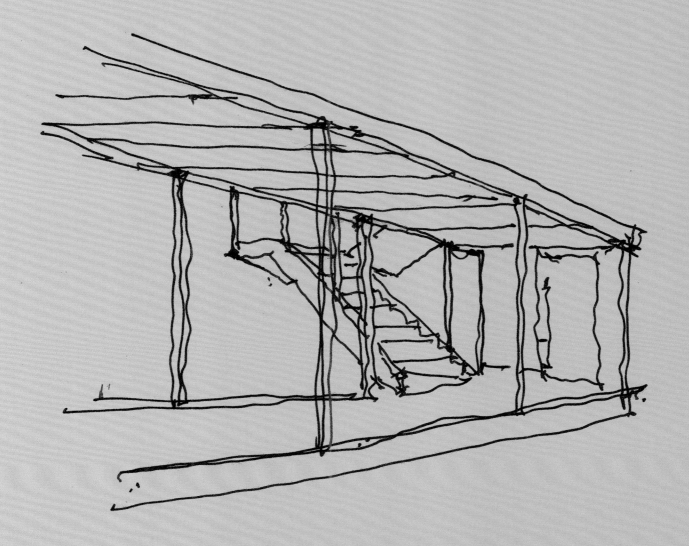

We made this house in Montecito for a couple who owns a property near our own. With their children grown, they were embarking on living full time in the country. They wanted a self-contained space that would work comfortably for the two of them alone, but which could be part of a flexible compound that would grow as their kids have families. It's a home intended for generations.

The arrangement of spaces started with the couple's main house at the top of the site. We added surrounding outbuildings to create a central outdoor living area. The hilly grade of the property dictated the loose, organic way the buildings were placed, in an angled L-shape around a lawn, and sloping down from it, a long, elegant pool. A huge, very old California oak tree in the middle of the grounds couldn't be moved, so we featured the tree as the heart of the property. With its slight elevation, it is the high ground that forms a view from every vantage point. From here, the ocean can be glimpsed to the south.

Because this is a full-time residence, the architecture is a bit more formal than in a vacation home. The couple are Francophiles with a home in France, and this property is, in its way, a rustic and modern interpretation of the country life they love in Provençe. A vernacular of stone country barns contributes to the old world feeling we were after. Inside and out, there's a good deal of panelized woodwork on doors and across cabinetry. Rooms have vaulted and beamed ceilings. Pristine white plaster balances the earthy stonework to define the modern aspects of the house. This white envelope gives the interiors a crisp, washed, dressier brightness. We used a set of restful French grey tones to create depth for the cabinetry, tile, and paint finishes, along with substantial slabs of beautiful French marble and limestone flooring.

The main house is simplified so that the couple don't feel they're rattling around in too big a space. It contains a spacious great room, combining the kitchen, living, and dining areas; a library; and a master suite reached by a private hallway. Another hallway connects to the tall garage with a floor of guest quarters upstairs. There's a guest cottage by the pool for more family. We made a separate stone barn as an art studio for the wife, who is a highly accomplished painter.

The rolling slope down to the pool establishes the sense of being in open countryside. For heritage, we planted an allée of old-growth olive trees that connects the upper and lower sections of the property. A pergola with a bamboo roof takes after an arbor, adding shade and forming one of the open-air dining areas that the family frequently uses. Nearby, an old-fashioned swing is hung from the branches of the oak tree, awaiting grandchildren, and carefree days together outside.

Opposite The path to the front door frames a building of stone and stucco. The house balances modern forms with the traditional materials in provincial architecture from the south of France.

Following The property was planned around a large, existing central oak tree. The main house, guest quarters, a painting studio, and the pool are all situated on the perimeter of a gently sloping yard, with paths and terraces winding around gardens and a broad lawn.

Right: An *allée* of young olive trees off the main entrance leads to a stone-clad fountain, providing a linear, axial connection from the main house to the art studio, and on to the pool and guesthouse.

Opposite French landscape **(clockwise from top left)**: A path leads to the kitchen garden, with citrus trees, herbs, lavender, and vegetables laid out in symmetrical beds. An outdoor potting sink, built into a wall of the painting studio, aids in the maintenance of the gardens. A view of the outdoor dining area is framed by colorful Californian and Mediterranean plants. A Juliet balcony graces a stone wall outside the painting studio.

Above Old olive trees and layers of tonal green plantings frame the secluded path to the front door from the driveway. Guest rooms occupy the second floor; the ground level is the garage.

Following (left) A steel wall sculpture in the entryway anchors a view through an arcade of trees in the garden. **(right)** Up close, the artwork is framed by the lines of the steel-and-glass pivoting front door.

Previous The great room is anchored on one end by a towering, Santa Barbara sandstone fireplace. The beamed cathedral ceiling adds loft and detail. To the right is the breezeway that leads to the master bedroom.

Opposite The owners wanted a dining space that would be a daily part of the household. The dining table stands next to a retractable glass window facing the garden, for an indoor-outdoor experience that welcomes simple family meals as well as hosting friends.

Following The kitchen stands in a quadrant of the great room, with the main workspace facing windows for a pleasant view. Through the doorway is a butler's pantry, providing extra storage and workspace, without inconveniencing the main kitchen area.

Overleaf (left) Flat-paneled cabinetry and banks of open shelving, a marble-topped island, and rich, grey-painted woodwork mediate a balance between a traditional farmhouse kitchen and a more edited design approach. **(right)** Belgian grey tile is used as the backsplash to the range.

Opposite The transparent stair enclosure leads to the guest rooms and is part of the connecting glass passageway to the main house. An internal gravel courtyard includes several boulders moved from the garden.

Above Another glass breezeway creates a private entry to the master bedroom wing. An external passage or hall of this type allows people to walk from one building to another without giving the house a heavy or over-sized feel.

Above Grey tones give the master bath a modern, French classicism. The floor is French limestone and the creamy grey marble at the sink is also from France. For continuity, the cabinetry style and paint finish from the kitchen were closely translated to the custom vanity. Curved corners on the mirror, countertop, and vanity, along with the soft shape of the tub, contrast with the room's otherwise rectilinear geometry. The bath has a north-facing private courtyard, which gives the room a soft light all day.

Opposite The master bedroom has its own vaulted and beamed ceiling, and opens onto a private patio with a view. The height and light circulation give the feel of a grand space without a particularly large footprint. An outdoor fireplace sits just beyond, between this bedroom wing and the main building.

Previous Looking from the main house, a rolling lawn provides a central, green space in front of the art studio and the pool house. The garden is slightly loose and unstructured. The oak tree gives shelter to a favorite outdoor dining area.

Opposite The owner of the house is an accomplished painter. Her studio is modeled after a classic Provençal stone house. Large, double-barn doors open to provide ventilation and allow her to wheel a table with her work in and out. This stone is native to the area and was installed on site by a local mason.

Above The studio opens to a large, north-facing window for even, all-day light. A stairway leads to an office on the loft level, making use of the height of the space.

Previous The grand heritage oak on the property instantly became the heart of the compound. In the French style, we created a gravel pad around it, making an idyllic space for an outdoor table.

Above and opposite Seen from this viewpoint, the pool is surrounded by fragrant, freeform planting beds and a natural limestone deck. The Meyer lemon trees are frequently harvested for drinks and cooking.

Following The pool sits at the bottom of the sloping lawn. We took advantage of this natural terrain to create an especially long, sixty-five-foot expanse for lots of family swimming activity. With a wide pergola for shade and a table for games and snacking, this lower portion of the compound is a destination.

AVIGNON

This residence in the Los Angeles neighborhood of Brentwood is designed in the manner of a French provincial chateau. The client had seen our own home in Hancock Park and liked our interpretation of classical French style for modern California life. Their wish was to create a close relative of our house, with a slightly dressier, yet still peaceful expression, in both the architecture and interiors.

In composing the house, we developed pared-down variations of archetypal forms from old-world, country chateaux. A central hallway creates a long, uninterrupted view from the front entrance out to the backyard and the pool. Moving inward, receiving rooms open on either side—a library on the right and a dining room on the left. A lyrical oval staircase is located in front of a two-story steel window with a skylight above, bringing light into the core of the house. A sun-filled kitchen and breakfast room form a modern-scaled side wing, with a view onto another outdoor sitting area set amid a courtyard, and across from it, a guesthouse.

The character of the house is revealed in its delicate paneling language. Rooms are delineated with the type of finely crafted millwork and material detailing to be found in antique French homes. Walls are panelized and ceilings have decorative mouldings, coves, and beams that break up the scale of big spaces. Cabinetry is built with more graceful paneling, French moulding profiles, and elegant hardware, from the kitchen to the commode-style vanities in the bathrooms. Fireplaces add age with antique marble mantels that we collected for the house in France, particularly from the region around Versailles, and in a range of styles from the eighteenth and nineteenth centuries.

In this same lineage, we used pale grey, cerused, wide oak planks for the flooring, and soft bisque and blue-grey paint finishes to match rich charcoal-colored, paneled doors—our update of a classic French palette. Continuing to streamline, Kazuko designed much of the furniture in sympathy with later French modern style. Pieces have a chic but very finished air, handcrafted in lavish materials.

The large, friendly kitchen needed to be a loved and practical space for a family that gathers here to cook and entertain—not just a kitchen for show. Still, I wanted to make the kitchen feel occupied by furniture, not equipment. Both the island and a long wall of cabinetry satisfy this concept, fulfilling practical storage requirements without making the room bulky. And typically of today, the island, with its wide, marble countertop and seating, is the center of family life. It joins the family room and breakfast bay to form an extended, relaxed hosting area that flows out to the terrace and pool. That balance of antique heritage and modern living was the aim throughout this house. And we continue to explore this mix of French and California ideas for many of our clients.

Opposite Italian cypress trees classically frame the front door. The contrasting plaster colors of the façade provide dimension and detail without needing more elaborate ornamentation or carving that would distract from the quiet balance of the house.

Following French provincial gardens provided inspiration for the landscape around the house. We emphasized the sculptural volumes of hedges and rounded topiary in varying shades of green, along with a formal reflecting pool. The organic shapes of old-growth olive trees relax the overall feeling and give the house a local context.

Previous The study is traditionally and fully paneled in custom-stained oak for a warm, old-world elegance. The eighteenth-century fireplace mantel is French Regency. We collected many of the mantels for the house from the region around Versailles.

Above The striated wall covering in the dining room reminded us of agate and was inspired by geological patterns. The surface of this unique paper echoes a textured plaster. We purposely left the room minimal to let the walls have the primary effect. Ceiling corners are rounded with a light, French arabesque line of moulding, to give the space even more prettiness. The Sputnik chandelier is vintage.

Opposite Moulding profiles, doors, and casings throughout the house are classical in form. We gave them a tailored finish, combining slate blue-grey and white paint colors with bisque-ivory walls. The living room fireplace is eighteenth-century French, of grey marble with brass accents. The glass sconces are Lalique-inspired.

Previous A bright bay window opens the living room to the backyard. The slender, tall proportions and fine paneling of the doors and windows are all characteristically French, though scaled up to feel more modern and let more light into the house. Restored modern furniture from the 1940s keeps the mood understated and polished.

Above The family room enjoys views of the trees and the pool. This space is symmetrical in form and detailing to the living room on the other side of the main hall. The eighteenth-century French limestone mantel was chosen to match the slightly less dressy, more domestic personality of this room, while still incorporating an antique feeling. Smooth, plaster panels are set flush around a television, minimizing the exposed technology in the room.

Opposite A built-in bar window neatly occupies an alcove in the family room and is accessible via the hallway to the dining room. The space is anchored by a custom demilune bar in olive burlwood finished with brass. The pair of tall wingback leather settees are our design.

Previous In the kitchen, Bianco Rhino marble clads the walls as well as the countertops. A complementary, rich grey marble pairs with the dark ebony of the island cabinetry. Here as in most of the house, we favored interesting light fixtures over recessed down-lighting. To avoid a pure period feeling, we used a mix of industrial drop pendants in antiqued brass over the sinks with belle-époque-style, pleated black silk shades over the island.

Opposite The breakfast room opens up to the garden through steel doors, providing one of the light-filled indoor-outdoor connections in the house. The leather chairs and the brass and textured lacquer table were custom-designed for the space. The durable lacquer was chosen to echo vintage goatskin furniture of the 1940s.

Above A gravel courtyard between the breakfast room and guesthouse serves as a relaxed entertaining and dining area. This space is inspired by garden locations in Provence. Rose bushes and citrus trees provide fragrance year-round.

Following A generous wall of cabinetry for dishes and servingware takes the form of a room-height French breakfront up on tapered legs. We loved the addition of this pale French blue paint finish to the house's overall palette. The special cabinetwork extends to paneled doors that cover the refrigerators. A hall of storage and the food pantry are behind the French doors, leading also to the bar in the family room.

Previous (left) A two-story brass-and-steel casement window illuminates the entry hall. The staircase is designed to be airy and graceful, crafted in fine finishes with a custom walnut, steel, and brass banister. **(right)** Upstairs, a skylight with a decorative metalwork diffuser brings more natural, ambient light to the entire volume of the hall as well as the passage to the bedrooms.

Above For the master bedroom, walls of framed paneling were simplified from the ornate French tradition, and lined with a quiet silver leaf finish. A minimal chandelier forms the juxtaposition of modernism and tradition that recurs throughout the house.

Opposite (left) In the master bath, the shower is entirely encased in bookmatched limestone. This beautiful stone is also used for the door and window casings and in large slabs for the floors. All the metalwork for the shower doors and mirror frames is custom-made in nickel. **(right)** Tucked into a cased opening with a tailored fit, a commode-style vanity is based on classic French furniture. The nickel-clad tub is centered in front of the window, for a peaceful view of the backyard.

Following (left) The main hall opens onto a covered loggia with a fireplace and indoor-outdoor seating. Continuing this long line, olive trees arc over the pool. Their close planting in lieu of a deck accentuates the garden setting and suggests the traditional character of a reflecting pool. The rear boundary wall is planted with cypress trees to create the feeling of an established villa landscape. Both effects are useful on a property without a wide natural vista. **(right)** Symmetry defines the view from the front entry through to the swimming pool, all aligned on the center axis of the house.

Overleaf Balconies, bays, and balustrades contribute to the clean yet classical architecture of the house. In particular, the pair of squared bay windows extends the traditional paneled style of the interior.

FLIGHT

The heart of this new modern house in Pacific Palisades was to serve a creative couple as they transitioned into working less and traveling more. They had raised their kids in a 1920s Spanish colonial house in Santa Monica; for this new residence, they didn't need a big family household and didn't want to walk past empty bedrooms.

The husband is a gourmet food purveyor and a serious wine collector, and the wife is a gourmet cook; so, a significant kitchen and a wine room had to be primary. The wife is also an artist and she needed a studio, but preferably apart from the house, so it could be a retreat for her.

In an extra twist, local zoning laws required houses in this neighborhood to have mostly pitched roofs to maintain continuity with the surrounding traditional architecture. So, we had to come up with a scheme that had sloping rooflines, without using classic gables. Floating planes of metal roofing came about to provide the imposed gradients. Simulating wings in flight as they ascend above glass-encased rooms, they turned out to be one of the best things about the house.

Early on we also needed to solve for where to site the painting studio in relation to the main house. Originally, it seemed logical to place a studio in the backyard. But on this fairly compact and tapered lot, putting another building there interfered with the harmony of the pool and the terrace as extensions of the living space. Then I realized that the studio could be designed as a kind of sculpture, an irregular shape in the house's big entry courtyard—like a boulder in the Ryoan-ji rock garden in Kyoto. That decision led to the idea of interpreting this outdoor space as an ode to Japan, and the sheltered front court quickly became a meditative gravel rock garden.

Inside, the couple wanted to simplify down to casual, one-room living. Much like a loft, the main floor is occupied by a wide, multi-purpose great room and kitchen. The full space opens onto a shaded terrace and the pool. This large main room in turn sets up the spacious master suite on top of it that rises to reveal the sky with a perimeter of clerestory windows. Peripheral rooms off this core include guest suites for the couple's children or visitors, a gym, an office, and, below, a full wine cellar and a comfortable screening room. This is all done with a minimum of internal hallways.

As part of the flow for both entertaining and home life, the large kitchen was designed for the wife and for professional-grade cooking. We partitioned the space with a glassed-in wine room that acts as a visual art piece as well as a dividing wall. Here as in the rest of the house, the finishes are practical, modern, and very durable. And, everything is tailored to exactly how the wife likes to cook. Even the island countertop was made a few inches below normal height, all bespoke and measured out for her.

Opposite The entry to the house is reached through a courtyard carpeted with large Mexican beach pebbles. The space was inspired by Japanese rock gardens and is bordered by Japanese plantings; the art studio to the left forms a sculptural monolith, like a boulder to contemplate in the garden.

Following The various sloped planes of the roof are visible from the front of the house. Board-form concrete and steel paneling, along with glass, are the major building materials. This palette was chosen not only for aesthetics, but also for weather resistance and low maintenance. The owners wanted materials that would require little upkeep for the times when they plan to be traveling.

Opposite In the courtyard, the pattern of rocks looks organic but it's not random. Thinner pebbles were set on edge to provide subtle patterning and rhythm.

Above A long, horizontal window in the studio provides a view of the fountain from the artist's desk.

Following (left) The corner window provides extra light in the easel's location. **(right)** Inside the studio the sloped ceilings echo the rooflines of the house, but as skylights, they provide the classically slanted, high, diffused light that is ideal for painting. The special low-lead glass provides for true color rendition for the artist.

Above An interior courtyard extends around the entry to the main house, with the same Japanese garden elements throughout. Various boulders are part of the tranquil setting; a Japanese maple tree provides color. The art studio left of the entry has an irregular shape that is meant to evoke a large boulder. The structure is clad in low-maintenance, black aluminum panels, emphasizing the form. A tall doorway opens to the courtyard for private passage to and from the house.

Opposite Visible from the front path, the house's main stairway is an elemental object itself. The floating steps are set against a sculptural wall that's made with a series of stacked, variable planks of bleached oak, similarly natural yet ordered.

Following A view from inside the entry. This is a double-height space that provides full visibility to the courtyard. We wanted to emphasize the uplifting structure of the house, allowing the use of glass and exposed steel framing to let the building feel as light as possible. The wood finishes add grounding so that the space doesn't feel cold.

Previous The great room encompasses all the main living quarters for the family. After the height of the entry, this space is wide and latitudinal, stretching to the open view of the backyard. Wood ceiling segments, varied in height, help to create separate, more-intimate areas within the whole for a living room, dining room, and bar, as well as a covered outdoor room with a barbecue for frequent lounging and dining.

Opposite As an artist, the lady of the house is particularly interested in shape and color, so together we selected a set of vivid furnishings to animate the architecture's neutral palette. A special rug enlivens the main seating area with broad, painterly brushstrokes of color, which remain visible through the custom glass-topped coffee table.

Above The fireplace column is clad in the same striated Chinese marble as the entry flooring, echoing the linear grain of the oak plank used throughout the house. An automated aluminum panel above the fireplace conceals a television. For additional seating, banquettes line the walls around the hearth to accommodate larger gatherings.

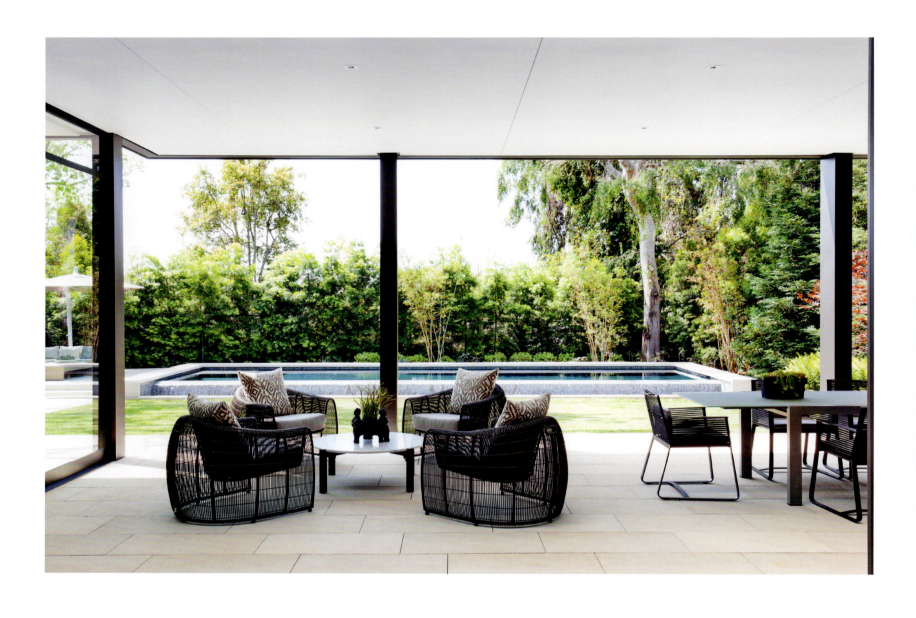

Above The covered patio outside the great room faces the swimming pool and beyond it, a stand of Japanese maples. The pool is made with a reverse infinity edge of glass tile, creating both a natural waterfall effect and a tranquil sound for the outdoor living areas.

Opposite In the dining room area, part of the husband's wine collection is showcased behind tinted glass doors—allowing a separate, conditioned wine cellar to become an artful and participatory display. Anticipating large to small gatherings, we chose two tables instead of one long one. Colorful chairs provide playful contrast and can be easily moved. The randomized series of spun globe ceiling fixtures add to the dynamic feeling of the setting.

Following The eat-in kitchen is located behind the wine cellar wall, letting its activity remain out of sight during entertaining, and providing a dedicated, tailor-made space for serious cooking. The room looks onto tall stands of green foliage, joining it to the outdoors. The very large square island is made of bleached oak and here stone is applied to the walls in a landscape orientation.

Overleaf (left) In the small powder room, the walls are lined in an immersive honeycomb surface made of cast plaster. The room is lit from recessed lighting incorporated into the floors, creating a kind of otherworldly luminescence. **(right)** In the stair hall, the vertical, stained-oak planking is backlit, which produces a glow through the slightly open seams, especially at night. We chose this material and lighting to add warmth and to balance the stone and glass in the space.

Previous In the master bedroom, clerestory windows built under the sloped roofs provide an added canopy of light. The effect is to let the space feel as if it's open to the sky. A large, private patio wraps around the room in an L-shape, adding more outdoor leisure space. The custom-designed headboard and nightstands create an enclosure for the bed, while the low, pillowy armchairs and gentle ombré effect of the rug add softness.

Above A tall niche of maple cabinetry encloses the sink in the master bath, with ribbed ceramic tile framing it. The shower is behind the sink wall.

Opposite Sliding doors open to an adjacent seating area on the patio. For this section of the patio, a pergola with textured glass walls provides privacy from neighboring homes.

Following The back of the house is all glass, so that there's no visual separation between inside and outside.

William Hefner is a California-based architect and the founder of Studio William Hefner. The firm specializes in architecture, interior design, and landscape design for homes. Studio William Hefner also designs fine furniture, lighting, and hardware. William's work is widely published in magazines and design books in the United States as well as internationally. He is the author of two previous books, *California Homes* and *Chateau des Fleurs*. He lives in Los Angeles with his son.

ACKNOWLEDGMENTS

First and foremost, I want to thank the clients who allowed us to collaborate with them on the creation of these California homes. Their openness and enthusiasm certainly established the foundations for the special work we were able to achieve. Each one put a tremendous amount of trust in us, allowing us to take chances and try new ideas. I so value these relationships—they're one of the most satisfying parts of what I get to do every day. Over the years, it's been such a great reward to see our clients settle into their new homes at the end of such a long commitment and process; to see how the houses come to life when they are happily occupied. I count myself very fortunate to be called upon to do this work and to see how people's lives change. And I continue to learn from all of them.

I'm constantly grateful for our incredible team at the Studio. We've all grown so much in the many years of working together, and our results improve as we mature. My late wife, Kazuko; business partners Carla Vaga and Nathalie Aragno; my longtime colleagues Mark Imagawa, Michael Aquino, and Bob Irvine, as well as their talented, tireless design groups who continue to learn and develop with us: Jenny Truong, Silvia Sirbu, Erica Blue, Chen-I Wu, Patricia Pedraza Omana, Domiane Forte, Yonatan Pressman, Alan Hotchkiss, Pollyann Meyers, Jorge Marién, Mark Johnson, Peter Lee, Ross Antido, Dennis Hardesty, Darren Andre, Christos Gersos, Natalia Polunina, Ruhui Ho, Paris Swanson, Shushan Gezalyan, Melissa Dana, Dario Kuwabara, Connie Billips, Devin Juleff, Lea Teitelbaum, Peter Sehorsch, Chih Sun, Kyle Ramey, Calvin Irvine, Donna Grossman, Gabriela Moran, Wayne Falcon, Nathan Zamero, Todd Ball, Tara Jepsen, and Amanda Tate Beir.

We are equally lucky to collaborate with a number of leading interior designers for some of these projects—I so enjoy these relationships. I would particularly like to thank the many fantastic craftspeople and vendors who are entrusted with the responsibility of bringing these homes to completion—more than I can mention, and all so devoted to their trades—from remarkable woodworkers, metalworkers, and stonemasons to wise horticulturists and arborists; fine gilders and leathersmiths to custom furniture makers and seasoned builders. Their expertise, focus, and care are crucial to our process.

PROJECT CREDITS

Designation: Trousdale
Location: Beverly Hills, CA
Architecture: William Hefner, Carla Vaga, Karen Fine
Landscape: William Hefner, Darren Andre
Interiors: Kazuko Hoshino, Jenny Truong
Contractor: RT Abbott Construction, Inc.
Photography: James Ray Spahn

Designation: Romero Canyon
Location: Montecito, CA
Architecture: William Hefner, Michael Aquino, Robert Irvine
Landscape: William Hefner, Darren Andre
Interiors: Kazuko Hoshino, Erica Blue, Jenny Truong, Silvia Sirbu
Contractor: Building Construction Group
Photography: Laura Hull

Designation: Beverly Hills
Location: Beverly Hills, CA
Architecture: William Hefner, Mark Imagawa, Jorge A. Marién
Landscape: William Hefner, Dennis Hardesty, Ruhui Ho
Interiors: Kazuko Hoshino, Silvia Sirbu, Wayne Nathan
Contractor: JD Group, Inc.
Photography: Laura Hull, Richard Powers

Designation: Canyon Farmhouse
Location: Los Angeles, CA
Architecture: William Hefner, Nathalie Aragno
Landscape: William Hefner, Darren Andre, Christos Gersos
Antiques, artifacts and design pieces: Galerie Provenance
Contractor: Synergy General Contractors
Photography: Laura Hull, Richard Powers

Designation: Wilshire
Location: Los Angeles, CA
Architecture: William Hefner, Nathalie Aragno
Interiors: Kazuko Hoshino, Silvia Sirbu, Erica Blue
Contractor: Randy Rudnick of Ralley Capital & Development
Photography: Roger Davies

Designation: New London
Location: Beverly Hills, CA
Architecture: William Hefner, Nathalie Aragno, Alan Hotchkiss
Landscape: William Hefner, Darren Andre, Ruhui Ho
Interiors: Antonia Hutt Interiors
Contractor: Hanover Builders, Inc.
Photography: Richard Powers

Designation: Palisades Ranch
Location: Pacific Palisades, CA
Architecture: William Hefner, Nathalie Aragno, Michael Aquino
Landscape: William Hefner, Darren Andre
Interiors: Annette English Assoc.
Contractor: Tyler Development
Photography: Erhard Pfeiffer, Richard Powers

Designation: Hot Springs
Location: Montecito, CA
Architecture: William Hefner, Michael Aquino, Robert Irvine
Landscape: William Hefner, Darren Andre, Ruhui Ho
Interiors: Catherine Bailly Dunne
Contractor: John Madden Construction
Photography: Laura Hull

Designation: Avignon
Location: Brentwood, CA
Architecture: William Hefner, Nathalie Aragno, Maria Iwanicki
Landscape: William Hefner, Darren Andre
Interiors: Kazuko Hoshino, Erica Blue, Silvia Sirbu
Contractor: Building Construction Group
Photography: Laura Hull

Designation: Flight
Location: Pacific Palisades, CA
Architecture: William Hefner, Nathalie Aragno, Michael Aquino
Landscape: William Hefner, Darren Andre
Interiors: Kazuko Hoshino, Jenny Truong
Contractor: Horizon General Contractors, Inc.
Photography: Roger Davies

Published in Australia in 2023 by
The Images Publishing Group Pty Ltd
ABN 89 059 734 431

Offices

Melbourne

Waterman Business Centre
Suite 64, Level 2 UL40
1341 Dandenong Road
Chadstone, VIC 3148
Australia

Tel: +61 3 8564 8122

New York

6 West 18th Street 4B
New York, NY 10011
United States

Tel: +1 212 645 1111

Shanghai

6F, Building C, 838 Guangji Road
Hongkou District, Shanghai 200434
China

Tel: +86 021 31260822

books@imagespublishing.com
www.imagespublishing.com

Copyright © Studio William Hefner (Text by Lisa Light) 2023
The Images Publishing Group Reference Number: 1669

All photography is attributed in the Project Credits on pages 294–295, unless otherwise noted.
Front cover: Firooz Zahedi (Romero Canyon); page 2: Laura Hull (Romero Canyon); page 6: Roger Davies (Flight); page 9: Richard Powers (Beverly Hills); page 291: Laura Hull (William Hefner)

All rights reserved. Apart from any fair dealing for the purposes of private study, research, criticism or review as permitted under the Copyright Act, no part of this publication may be reproduced, stored in a retrieval system or transmitted in any form by any means, electronic, mechanical, photocopying, recording or otherwise, without the written permission of the publisher.

Title: California Homes II (new edition) // Studio William Hefner
ISBN: 9781864709490

This title was commissioned in IMAGES' Melbourne office and produced as follows:
Editorial Georgia (Gina) Tsarouhas, Danielle Hampshire, Jeanette Wall, *Graphic design & production* Nicole Boehringer

Printed on 157gsm OJI matt art paper by Artron Art Group in China

IMAGES has included on its website a page for special notices in relation to this and its other publications.
Please visit www.imagespublishing.com

Every effort has been made to trace the original source of copyright material contained in this book.
The publishers would be pleased to hear from copyright holders to rectify any errors or omissions.
The information and illustrations in this publication have been prepared and supplied by Studio William Hefner and the participants. While all reasonable efforts have been made to ensure accuracy, the publishers do not, under any circumstances, accept responsibility for errors, omissions and representations express or implied.